**THE BRITISH
HORSE SOCIETY**

CW00516152

EXMOOR ON HORSEBACK

AVAILABLE IN THIS SERIES

The Cotswolds on Horseback
Wiltshire on Horseback
Westmorland on Horseback
The Ridgeway Downs on Horseback
Exmoor on Horseback
Somerset on Horseback
Hampshire on Horseback
Leicestershire on Horseback

First published 1994
by The British Horse Society
Access & Rights of Way Department
British Equestrian Centre
Stoneleigh Park, Kenilworth
Warwickshire CV8 2LR

A catalogue record for this book is available from the British Library

ISBN 1 899016 01 5

Printed by:
Tripod Press Limited, 7 Wise Street, Leamington Spa, CV31 3AP

Distribution: The British Horse Society, Stoneleigh Park, Kenilworth,
Warwickshire, CV8 2LR

CONTENTS

ACKNOWLEDGEMENTS

A number of people and organisations have given their time and expertise to provide details for this guide book.

In particular, the British Horse Society would like to thank Anna Baness who surveyed and described the routes and Philippa Luard for writing the Introduction.

FOREWORD

The '.................. on Horseback' series of published rides launched in 1993 has proved extremely popular. This confirms the British Horse Society's belief that many riders need information on routes known to be open, available and providing pleasurable riding.

Many volunteers have worked to research these routes, thus helping to contribute to the Countryside Commission's target of having all rights of way defined, open and signed by the year 2000. This Society wholeheartedly supports this aim which it incorporates into its Access & Rights of Way strategy for the last decade of this Century.

Together with our booklet 'Bed & Breakfast for Horses', these publications enable riders and carriage drivers to plan holidays and other trips. This extends the pleasure and value of owning a horse either to ride or drive, and enables an assortment of different experiences to be enjoyed be they landscape, flora and fauna or historic sites and buildings.

Equestrianism provides one of the most intense pleasures of life, wholly understood only by those who ride or drive carriages. The Society is proud to contribute in some way to the fulfilment of that pleasure. The challenges of research and development of further routes will continue to be explored.

E A T BONNOR-MAURICE
Chairman, British Horse Society

March 1994

INTRODUCTION

The British Horse Society's ARROW Project aims to identify open and usable routes of varying length and shape (circular, figure-of-eight or linear) to help riders and carriage drivers to enjoy the countryside by means, as far as possible, of the network of public rights of way and the minor vehicular highways. This collection of rides is the result of research and mapping by volunteers who took up the challenge of the ARROW initiative with such enthusiasm and effort.

I am faced with the equally daunting challenge of writing an introductory chapter. Should I write reams about each topic or try simply to point you in the right direction? I have decided upon the second method as the search for information is itself highly educative and stays in the mind better than reading it all in one place. Also, since we all have different expectations of our holiday, a very full guide seemed wrong. Nevertheless, there are a few pointers I would like to suggest to you.

The most important one is to start your planning several months in advance of the trip, including a visit to the area you intend to ride in. You should make endless lists of things to DO (e.g. get the saddle checked) and things to CHECK OUT (can you read a map, for instance). You may find joining the local BHS Endurance Riding Group very helpful, as there you will meet people who can give you information about the degree of fitness needed for yourself and your horse (feeding for fitness not dottiness) , and many other useful hints on adventurous riding. You may also enjoy some of the Pleasure rides organised by the group or by the local Riding Club. These are usually about 15-20 miles and you ride in company,

though using a map. You may find them under the title Training Rides. These rides will get both of you used to going into strange country. If you usually ride on well-known tracks, then your horse will find it nerve-racking to go off into new territory, and you yourself may also find the excitement of deep country a bit surprising, so try to widen your experience at home before you go off on holiday.

ACCOMMODATION

Decide how far you wish to ride each day of your holiday, book overnight accommodation for both of you and if possible visit it to see if the five-star suite on offer to your horse is what he is used to Decide if you want to stable him or to turn him out at the end of the day, and arrange to drop off some food for him, as he will not relish hard work on a diet of green grass nor will he enjoy a change in his usual food. If you are to have a back-up vehicle of course, then you will not need to do some of this, but you should certainly make a preliminary visit if you can. The BHS publish a Bed & Breakfast Guide for Horses which is a list of people willing to accommodate horses, and sometimes riders, overnight. The Society does not inspect these places, so you should check everything in advance.

FITNESS

You and your horse should be fit. For both of you , this is a process taking about two months. If you and/or your horse are not in the full flush of youth, then it may take a bit longer. The office chair, the factory floor, or the household duties do not make or keep you fit, but carefully planned exercise will. Remember that no matter how fit your horse seems, he does not keep himself fit - you get him fit. There are several books with details of fitness programmes for a series of rides. Do not forget to build in a rest day during your holiday - neither of you can keep going all the time, day after day. Miles of walking may get you fit, but it uses different muscles from riding; you may get a surprise when you start riding longer distances. It seems to me that the further you intend to ride, the longer your preparation should be. Nothing can be done in a hurry.

Your horse should be obedient, so work on that. If you want him to stand, then he must stand. If you want to go through water, then he must be prepared to walk down a slope or even step down off a bank to go through the stream, so start with puddles and insist that he go through the middle. Does he help you open gates? I hope so, or you will have a great deal of mounting and dismounting to do. Does he tie up - this is essential if you are to have a peaceful pint at lunchtime.

MAPS

Can you read a map? Can you make and read a grid reference (usually referred to as GR)? Get a Pathfinder map of your area and take yourself for a walk and see if you end up where you expect to. Learn to know exactly where you are on the map, and how to understand the symbols (if your map shows hilly ground, the journey will take longer). Can you work out how long a ride is in miles and roughly how long it will take? You will be using rights of way and it is very important that you stay in the line of the path - that is the only place you have a right to be, and you may deviate from that line only as much as is necessary to get you round an obstruction on the path. You are going to be riding over land that forms part of someone's work place and that fact must be respected. It is only by the efforts of farmers and landowners that the countryside exists in its present form - so that we may enjoy it as we pass by.

You will need to know the grid reference (GR.) of the start and end of the various tracks you are to use. Get a copy of an Ordnance Survey (OS) Landranger map and really learn the details on the right-hand side, some of which explain how to arrive at a Grid Reference. Learn to go in the door (Eastings - from left to right) and up the stairs (Northings - from bottom to top). There is a great deal of information on the Landranger maps and not so much on the Pathfinders, but the Pathfinder gives more details on the map itself, so that is the map you will use for the actual ride. Or you may care to buy a Landranger of the area you are visiting and, using a highlighter pen, mark in all the rides you want to make, so that you can see through the marks you make. Then get from any Outdoor shop a map case which will allow you to read the map without taking it out of the case and which you can secure round yourself. Also, you should know if you are facing north, south, east or west as you ride. Quite important if you think about it, as it is no good riding into the sunset if you are meant to be going south. Plastic orienteering compasses are cheap and reliable.

TACK

Have your tack thoroughly checked by your saddler, as there is nothing so annoying as a sore back which could have been prevented, or an unnecessarily broken girth strap. How are you going to carry the essential headcollar and rope each day? What about spare shoes, or a false shoe?

What to take on the ride depends on how much back-up you have. If you have to carry a change of clothes, etc., then you are into very careful planning indeed - balance saddle bag, the lot. If you are based at your first night stop all the time, then life is much easier. You should always carry a first aid kit for horse and rider. You will also have to plan how to wash the girth and numnah. Remember our delightful climate and always carry a waterproof and additional warm clothing - it never pays to gamble with rain and wind.

SAFETY

It is always wiser to ride in company. The other person can always hold your horse, or pull you out of the ditch, as well as being someone to talk to about the excitements of the day and to help plan everything. You should always wear a BSI riding hat, properly secured, and also safe footwear. You need a clearly defined heel and a smooth sole. Even if riding in company, tell someone where you are going and roughly how long you expect to take. If affordable, take a portable telephone. Make a list of the things you must carry every day and check it before leaving base.

INSURANCE

You should have Third Party Legal Liability Insurance. This will protect you if you or your horse cause a bit of mayhem (accidentally!). Membership of the BHS gives you this type of insurance, plus Personal Accident Insurance as part of the membership package. Check your household insurance to make sure it covers riding before you rely only on that, as some insurances do not. You should always have this type of cover when venturing forth into the outside world, even if it is an hours hack from home.

PARKING

If you intend to box to the start of the day's ride, either have someone to take the box away or make sure it is safely, securely and considerately parked. If you have to make arrangements to park, do it well in advance or the contact may well have gone,to market or the hairdressers when you make a last minute call. Have the vehicle number etched on to the windows for security.

MONEY

This is vital, so work out a system of getting money if necessary. Sadly we can no longer gallop up to the bank and lead Dobbin into the cashier's queue, nor do most banks have hitching rails. Post Offices are more numerous and might be a useful alternative. Always have the price of a telephone call on you.

Lastly, if you do run into problems of blocked paths or boggy ones, write to the Highway Authority of the relevant county council and tell them. Then you can do something about it. You might even think of adopting a path near home and keeping an eye on it, telling your own county council of any difficulties you encounter. It is through such voluntary work that these rides have been made possible.

Wherever you ride, always do it responsibly, with care of the land, consideration for the farmer and courtesy for all other users. Remember the Country Code and enjoy your ARROW Riding.

I hope this chapter will have started you planning and making lists. If I seem to be always writing about forward planning it is only because I usually leave things to the last minute, which causes chaos!

PHILIPPA LUARD

EXMOOR

Straddling the boundary between Devon and Somerset is a high plateau taking its name from the River Exe, which rises there.

Along the coast are England's highest sea cliffs, revealing hazy views of Welsh mountains.

From the plateau run rivulets, which seem benign but can burst into torrents, etching the landscape with steep little combes. These separate the rounded hillsides and heath-topped ridges and in them nestle ancient woodlands and equally ancient farmsteads.

The highest ridge culminates in the 1704 feet Dunkery Beacon, a name reflecting former times when smoke or fire were the most rapid way of passing messages or warning of danger. The area has been settled since the 7th Century BC and the whole landscape reflects its history. Many place names date from Celtic times when Welsh was the local language.

The moorland is fragmented. The motorist would be forgiven for missing it altogether, as much was enclosed over the last two centuries with Beech topped hedgebanks, which line wide-verged enclosure roads' obscuring many fine views waiting to be discovered by the rider.

The hedgebanks are the stitching in the patchwork of small fields which provide pasture for sheep and beef cattle. The dried leaves of autumn shelter the stock from winter winds and drifting snow.

With the low winter sun behind them they come alive again with russets, ochres and gold until they are ousted by the downy olive leaflets of spring.

Sheep farming has been the mainstay of the area's economy from early medieval times and has been important since the Bronze Age, 3500 years ago. It has largely been responsible for Exmoor's landscape as we know it today. The moorland itself partly results from the grazing of sheep preventing the regeneration of natural woodlands. Periodic burning or swaling to provide fresh grazing also helps to prevent regrowth of trees.

The heyday of the sheep on Exmoor was probably in medieval times, when the woollen industry was at its height. Many of today's bridleways developed, along with tiny stone bridges, as routes for the packhorses carrying wool and cloth, although several have been in use since prehistoric times. Until the 19th Century the moorland was used for summer grazing only and many ancient routes developed as drove roads for seasonal movements of stock for grazing or market.

The moors and heaths offer quiet recreation and chance for solitude, shared with the red deer, wild ponies and buzzards for which Exmoor is famous. These are truly wild animals and not easily approached, but more easily on horseback as the horse does not appear as a threat. The buzzards and deer can be seen everywhere, although the latter are more common to the east and south of Exmoor and are seen in the open more at dusk and dawn. The ponies are confined to particular areas of moorland. Those crossed by these routes are at Brendon Common, Bradymoor, Winsford Hill, Warren and Lucott Moor.

The ponies are few in number - less than 750 worldwide and only about 200 remaining on the moor. They arrived during the Ice Age, migrating with the seasons and the advance and retreat of the ice sheets whilst Britain was still joined to the continent. They lived on grasslands throughout the northern hemisphere and were amongst the original horses to be domesticated. They were probably never particularly numerous on Exmoor, but through the vagaries of history this was the only place where they survived.

From Norman times until the early 19th Century they were protected as wild animals within the Royal Forest, the ancient moorland heart of Exmoor. Then the Forest was sold by the Crown to a businessman and the handful of good ponies remaining were only saved through the interest of Sir Thomas Acland, the former Warden of the Forest. The ponies were branded with his family symbol, an anchor, and the Anchor herd became the foundation for all present stock. Now there are several herds, including two owned by the National Park Authority, and inspection and registration are controlled through the Exmoor Pony Society.

The moorland plateau was little known until the end of the 18th Century. Touring the area in the 16th Century, Leland described it as a 'barren and moorish ground' and two centuries later Defoe said of Exmoor: 'Camden calls it a filthy, barren ground, and, indeed, so it is'. Porlock was then described as 'the end of the world' as, approaching from the east, Exmoor beyond was impenetrable for wheeled traffic. Indeed, horseback was the only form of transport on most of Exmoor until well into the 19th century and goods were carried in panniers or dragged behind on poles or sleds. Sturdy Exmoor ponies were much in demand breeding stock for pack horses. Following the industrial and agricultural revolutions they were much in demand for carrying ores from Exmoor's mines and lime from the coast for moorland reclamation or for pit ponies elsewhere.

Today we have a different view of the landscape, which owes much to the Romantic Movement in the arts in the late 18th and early 19th centuries. At that time visitors such as Wordsworth, Coleridge and Shelley came to the Exmoor coast for the inspiration of the landscape. Thousands followed and changed the economy of the area. Roads and railways were developed, but it was a long time before motor vehicles were made powerful enough to cope with some of Exmoor's gradients. Horse drawn stagecoaches continued running along the main coast road until the 1920s. Visitors still had to walk up the steepest hills whilst their luggage was carried ahead.

The only tourist resort which developed within the area which became the National Park, however, is Lynton and Lynmouth and those attracted to beaches keep to the east and west of

Exmoor and the larger resorts of Minehead and Ilfracombe. Inland there are a few tourist 'honeypots' such as Oare and Malmsmead, famed for their connection with the 19th century novel 'Lorna Doone', Dunster with its castle and ancient bridge at Tarr Steps. But it is Exmoor which is the attraction for the rider and these are places to avoid at busy times as horses, traffic and narrow lanes do not mix. The majority of visitors do not wander far from their cars and for the rider much can be enjoyed in peace.

Exmoor has been described as 'the riding playground of England'. It is superb riding country and offers every facility for the rider. Riding stables are scattered over the whole area and most larger settlements have their tack shop, vet and farrier. The locals are heavily involved in equestrian culture. There is every sort of hunting, eventing, point to points, gymkhanas and shows. Notable are the Exmoor Spring Horse Show, Exmoor Pony Society Stallion Parade and Golden Horseshoe Ride, all in May, the Exmoor Carriage Driving Festival at the end of July and Brendon Pony Show in August. Bampton Fair developed around its Exmoor Pony sales. The ponies have now gone, but the fair still flourishes. The Minehead Hobby Horse parade has nothing to do with horses, but is an ancient May Day custom.

Exmoor National Park encompasses the moorland plateau plus the fertile Vale of Porlock and the farmed and forested Brendon Hills to the east. In all it covers 267 square miles - a large area, but small for a National Park. Forty years ago, its expanse of relatively open and unspoiled countryside was seen to offer great potential for quiet recreation, which led to its selection for special protection as one of our finest landscapes.

It remains protected for the nation's benefit, but not in the nation's ownership. Exmoor is not a museum, but a living landscape where over 10,000 people live and work. Much of the land is privately owned and it is largely the local farmers and landowners who manage the landscape. The National park Authority encourages them to do so in a manner conducive to the conservation and amenity of the area.

The Authority is responsible for the upkeep of rights of way, including bridleways. It pioneered the system of waymarking - the use of coloured symbols to help visitors follow certain routes. Originally, different colours were used for different routes, but now they denote status. At the time of writing in the spring of 1994, riders can use the blue and red coloured routes, but not the yellow ones; however from May 1994 all waymarking will comply with the national standard. Usually they are helpfully signposted as well, but a proliferation of signs and markers is avoided in open areas to maintain the feel of wilderness. Not all routes are waymarked but large sections of these ARROW routes are. They have been carefully selected to provide enjoyable rides whilst avoiding vulnerable areas, so please keep to the recommended tracks.

Small sections of these routes are permissive - where landowners have given their consent for public use, but where riders have no legal rights of way.

In this case consent has been given by the Forestry Commission and National Trust, who are major landowners on Exmoor. There are other permissive bridleways on their properties. Often they are signposted and waymarked, but not always and not all of their tracks are available to riders. In addition there are some parts of Exmoor where, partly through hunting interest, it is common practice to wander freely, but local knowledge is necessary to ride where this is acceptable and safe. It is wise to take advice and a guide, particularly on open moorland where boggy areas can provide difficulties for horse and rider.

Exmoor has been described as 'a seemingly soft and gentle place where the elements have combined to create a beautiful, fragile..... landscape'. It is for beauty, peace and being at one with nature, and for exploring - a place with many secrets. It is an area of great variety and, despite its small size, always has something new to offer. Once visitors have begun to explore on foot or horse they tend to return time and time again. These rides provide a taste of Exmoor and, we hope, a great deal of pleasure.

WILD ANIMALS IN NATIONAL PARKS
(A cautionary note!)

STALLIONS

Great Britain has a world envied heritage of native pony breeds scattered across the whole country. Anyone going on a riding holiday should be aware of the hazards they may encounter if they go where the native herds run wild on moorland, fells, dales and large commons. Stallions are very protective of their mares, particularly at foaling time in late spring and early summer - this is also mating time. A strange horse coming too close is either a threat to the stallion's territory, or a mare to be included in his harem. Not all stallions will depart over the horizon with their family when you appear, and you may find yourself in a very dangerous situation if the stallion decides to attack your horse. So it is wiser to keep well away. You can usually see the herd from a fair distance and take avoiding action, tempting though it may be to get closer to the charming scene. Remember they are wild ponies, living as naturally as the twentieth century permits, and should be left in peace. You are most likely to find the wild herds in such places as the Brecon Beacons and similar open moorland in Wales and large commons in the Lake District and the north of England. Across the south of England they are to be found on Exmoor, Dartmoor and in the New Forest. Some herds are out the whole year round, and others are brought down to better grazing during the winter months.

HUNTING AND DEER

Exmoor is renowned for its hunting. There are staghounds, foxhounds and beagles hunting regularly. From the visiting rider's point of view you should be aware that it is only during the months of May, June and July that no hunting takes place. At all other times you should be prepared to meet hounds, huntsmen and followers. There are also a great many car and motor-bike followers some of the latter going cross-country with horses. Be careful.

One thing to remember about the red deer is that the calves, born in May and June, are often hidden in the bracken for long periods of time. They are not abandoned and their mothers are nearby. If you do find one, do not stop or touch it. Just store up the memory, and keep going, secure in the knowledge that you have not disturbed mother or child. Another point to remember is that in the rutting season in October, the stags can become rather aggressive, and should be avoided, fascinating though their roaring, fighting and wallowing may be. Give them a wide berth for safety.

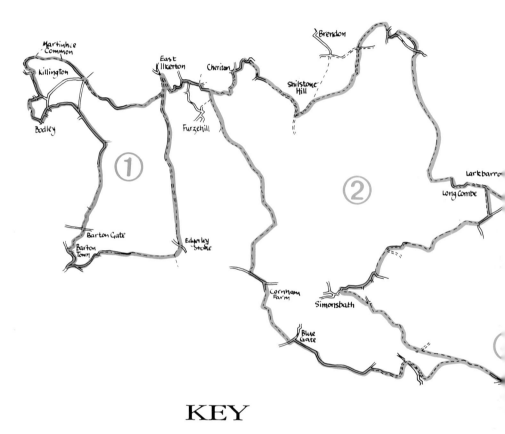

KEY

═════ ─ ─ ─   **ROADS**

+ + + + + + +   **BYWAYS**

─ ─ ─ ─ ─ ─   **BRIDLEWAYS**

14

EXMOOR
ON HORSEBACK

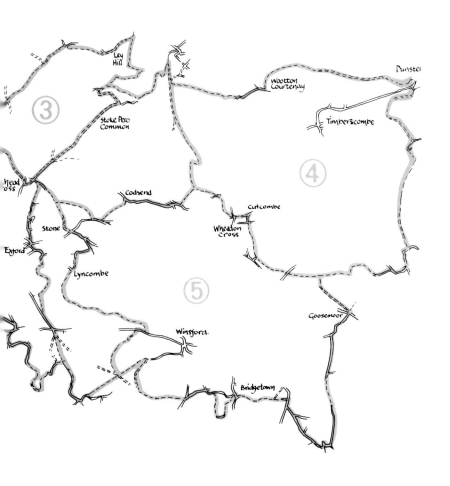

The Dell

Cowbridge, Timberscombe,
Minehead, Somerset TA24 7TD
Telephone: (0643) 841564

Bed & Breakfast in a charming 17th century house.**Bedrooms**:Three double one single, two with H/C, one with shower, one public bathroom.
Terms: From £14.50 to £17.50, reductions for children.
Stabling & paddock available.
ETB Listed. Ample parking, spacious gardens, lovely views, near to moorland and the sea.Tea and coffee making facilities, TV.
**PROPRIETORS:
HARRY AND SUE CRAWFORD**

Disclaimer

Whilst all due care was taken in the preparation of these maps neither the British Horse Society nor their agents or servants accept any responsibility for any inaccuracies which may occur. It should be borne in mind that landmarks and conditions change and it is assumed that the user has a Pathfinder or Landranger Ordnance Survey map and a compass.

SAFETY

Know your Highway Code (1994 Edition)

**In Particular
Paragraphs 216/224**

INSURANCE:

The BHS recommends that before undertaking any of these routes, both horse and rider be adequately insured against **THIRD PARTY PUBLIC LIABILITY.** Membership of the BHS gives automatic Third Party Insurance with an indemnity of up to £2,000,000.

TIMBERSCOMBE

A 21 MILE CIRCULAR TRAIL (CLOCKWISE)

Ordnance Survey Maps:
Landranger 181

Parking & Starting Points:
There is limited parking in the centre of Timberscombe. Your starting point is Great House Street, Timberscombe (GR.956421)

NOTE: This ride is through a variety of Exmoor scenery, open moorland, broadleaved and coniferous woodland, and farmland. There are some very steep hills as the route goes up and down the wooded combes and therefore it should only be tackled by a fit horse and rider!

There are ample 'watering holes' for horses along this route, but facilities for riders are not so plentiful. In order to be certain of food and drink, riders are advised to provide a packed meal.

Route Description:

. Ride from your parking place and take the first left out of Great House Street and follow the bridleway to Luxborough. Go straight across the first road (GR.969411) and keep going uphill along the main forestry track, ignoring any side turnings. Just before the top of the hill you will come to a six-way junction, turn right here downhill to Luxborough. At the first road junction (GR.985379), turn right then take the next right (GR.985379). Go through Luxborough and turn right (GR.984377)along the metalled road

signposted to Dunster. After 0.25 miles take the track on the left, signposted to Wheddon Cross. Ride down the track and cross the stream (GR.982371), then turn right (GR.982370)and right again (GR.981370) to leave the ponds (GR.978360) on your left. Follow the track along the hillside until you come to the fork just before the track drops downhill towards a cottage (GR.979369). Take the right fork and follow the waymarked path into the woods. Ride across the river through the ford and turn left to go uphill. At the next junction turn right (GR.973369). *Take care riding through these woods as the area is used for pheasant rearing and the young birds could startle your horse!* After a short distance turn left and follow the waymarked bridleway uphill to the fields. Go through the gate and turn right along the field side until you reach the next gate. (Approximately 4.50 miles)

2.	Go through the gate and onto the main forestry track where you turn right (GR.966363) and follow the track downhill. When you come to the stream (GR.963365) take the bridleway to your left and go uphill to follow the track through a plantation to come to the next forestry track (GR.964361). Turn left and at the next junction turn right to the car park on the top of Kennisham Hill (GR. 964358). Turn right and follow the forestry track straight on to fields. Ride thorough the gate and straight across the field leaving the barns on your left. At the next junction of paths

(GR.954371) turn left and follow the waymarkings through fields to come to a road (GR.943371). **PLEASE DO NOT GALLOP THROUGH THE FIELDS.** When you reach the road go straight across, *(you are now half way along your ride)* and follow the waymarked path past Pitleigh to Wheddon Cross (GR.930388). At the next road junction go straight on then take the next left (GR.929391). Continue along this road and where it bends sharp left, go through the gate (GR. 927391) and follow the hedge on the right until you come to a main road (A396). Ride straight across this road and follow the lane downhill taking the second right along the bridleway towards Raleigh Manor (GR.923391).

3.   Before you reach Raleigh Manor, turn right (GR.921394) and follow the bridleway through the woods keeping along the main track. *This track can get quite muddy at times so take it slowly.* At the next road go straight across and follow the bridleway through the woods and uphill to your right onto the open moor. Ride out to your right going uphill to meet a road (GR. 904425). Turn right along the road. *Above you to your left is Dunkery Beacon, the most famous landmark on the moor.*

4.   Ride along the road down to Webber's Post and turn left along the Dickies Path. *You get beautiful views of Dunkery Beacon on your left all the way along this path.* At the next road junction turn right (GR.878426) and then take the next left to Stoke Pero (GR.885430). Ride past the tiny church and turn right and ride through Church Farm farmyard and follow the bridleway through the fields to Cloutsham (GR.892431). At Cloutsham, turn left

and follow the bridleway down to cross the river at the ford and ride up the other side to the road (GR.903443). (Approximately 16.50 miles)

5.   At the road turn left and continue downhill to a cross-roads. Turn right along the track and then take the next right uphill to Webber's Post (GR.903436). At Webber's Post turn left and follow the Dunster Path to Brockwell. *On a clear day you get some lovely views across the valley to Selworthy and the hills along the coast from this path.* Keep following the main path until just before the woods and then turn downhill to your left (GR.922432). Follow the track down through the woods and into the lane between the fields until you come to a ford where you turn left. (GR.927431) and follow a track to the road.

TRAIL 1.

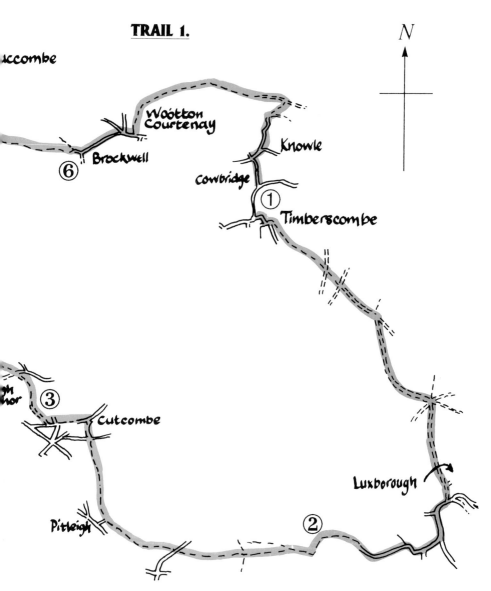

6. At the road turn left to Wootton Courtenay (GR.928431). At the next road junction turn right (GR.935434). Just before the houses, turn left uphill along the bridleway to Dunster (GR.937434). Ride along the main track for approximately one mile. When you come to the cross tracks, turn right to Timberscombe. Cross the next track and continue downhill to a road (GR.956431). At the road turn right and then take the next left. When you come to the main road (A396) *TAKE CARE, this road can be busy at times,* turn right back to Timberscombe and your starting point.

Rose Cottage, Dunster

21

THROUGH PARRACOMBE

A 22 MILE CIRCULAR TRAIL (CLOCKWISE)

Ordnance Survey Maps:
Landranger 180

Parking & Starting Point:
Parking is available at several car parks on the B3223 (GR.753461) which also forms the starting point.

NOTE: *There are ample 'watering holes' for horses along this route, but facilities for riders are not so plentiful. In order to be certain of food and drink, riders are advised to provide a packed meal.*

Route Description:

1.   From the starting point ride downhill to your right along the bridleway that leads down through the farmland (GR.748462) to Farley Water Farm entrance (GR.745464). Turn right and follow the lane for a short distance, then at the sharp bend turn left along the bridleway downhill through the woods (GR.746465), to a road. At this road turn left and follow it through Bridge Ball. Take the next road left uphill to Cheriton, then take a track to the left after the first farm on the left (GR.737466). Where this track forks take the bridleway which is the right-hand fork, and follow the bridleway across Hoaroak Water to Stock Common (GR.729459) leaving Roborough Castle, *which is an ancient settlement,* on your right. From Stock Common follow the track down to the road (GR.722463) and turn right. Where the road bends sharply to the right turn left along the lane signposted to Sparhanger Farm. Follow the lane across the river and up to the moor on the other side. On the open moor turn right along the track to a road (GR.711465). Turn left along this road and follow it to Shallowford (GR.714449). Continue straight on along the track for one mile to Saddle Gate (GR.715435). (Approximately 4.50 miles).

2.   From Saddle Gate follow the grassy track straight on up and over the hill heading for the beacon on the horizon (GR.716425). *BEWARE of wet areas on the top of the hill.* Go through the gate which is on the left of the beacon and follow the track down to the main road (B3358), staying parallel with the wall on your right. *There are wonderful views from the top here as you ride across Winaway and Broad Mead.*

At the B3358, go straight across and follow the track uphill on the other side. When you come to a T-junction (GR.716405), turn right and follow the bridleway to Challacombe. Keep riding parallel with the wall on your right and then go diagonally downhill to the right to come to a track..

3.   Follow the track down to a road and turn left (GR.691407). *(As you are now almost half way into your ride, you may wish to stop for refreshments. If so, instead of turning left, turn right*

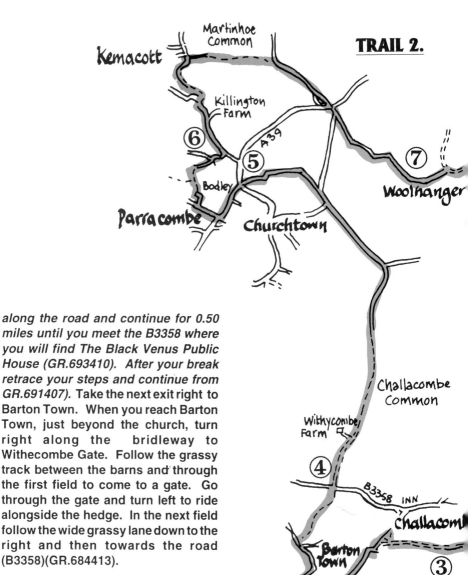

along the road and continue for 0.50 miles until you meet the B3358 where you will find The Black Venus Public House (GR.693410). After your break retrace your steps and continue from GR.691407). Take the next exit right to Barton Town. When you reach Barton Town, just beyond the church, turn right along the bridleway to Withecombe Gate. Follow the grassy track between the barns and through the first field to come to a gate. Go through the gate and turn left to ride alongside the hedge. In the next field follow the wide grassy lane down to the right and then towards the road (B3358)(GR.684413).

4.   At the road (B3358), turn left and then almost immediately turn right up a lane signposted to Withycombe Farm. Where the lane bends sharp left, keep riding straight on up through the fields (GR.686419) and on reaching the moor, follow a grassy track straight on to the top of the next lane (GR.690434). Go through the gate and follow the lane for two miles down to a main road (A39).

5.   Ride straight across the main road (A39)(GR.672454) and take the minor road signposted to Parracombe. At the first crossroads turn right signposted to Bodley. At the end of the road take the bridleway on the right and follow it round to the right to the next road (GR.670458).

24

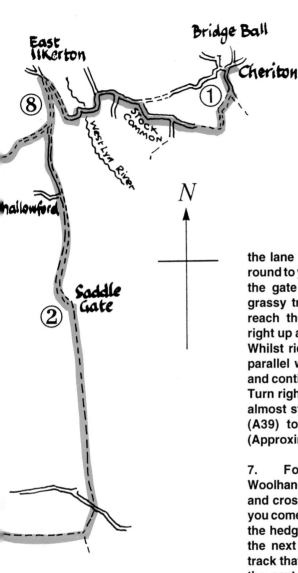

the lane (GR.667466) follow the track round to your left to a gate. Go through the gate into a field and follow the grassy track straight on. When you reach the houses (GR.665471), turn right up a lane to Martinhoe Common. Whilst riding through the fields, stay parallel with the hedge on your right and continue until you come to a road. Turn right along the road and then go almost straight across the main road (A39) to Woolhanger (GR.685464). (Approximately 18 miles).

7.   Follow the lane through Woolhanger (GR.698454) and turn right and cross the river at the ford. When you come to the end of the track, follow the hedge on your right. Go through the next gate and follow the grassy track that swings out to the left. After the next gate, follow the stony track down across the river to Thornworthy Farm (GR.710457). At the farm, turn right and ride along the entrance track to the road along Ilkerton Ridge.

8.   On reaching a road (GR.712459), turn left and retrace your steps through Cheriton and Bridge Ball to your starting point.

.   When you meet the road, turn eft and ride along to pass Killington ⁻arm. *TAKE CARE as there are blind bends in the road and beware of the steep bend below Killington - the road surface provides little grip for horses.* Just before you reach the river, turn ight along the bridleway to Martinhoe Common and Kemacott. At the end of

25

Malmsmead Bridge

SIMONSBATH

TRAIL 3

A 27 MILE CIRCULAR TRAIL (CLOCKWISE)

Ordnance Survey Map:
Landranger: 180 &181

Starting Point:
Parking is available in a layby on the B3223 (GR.776393). The start of your ride is from GR .773392 (Simonsbath)

NOTE: This trail takes you through Lorna Doone country with views of Badgworthy Water running through Doone Country, and of Oare Church. It is the longest circular ride in this area and the hills are quite steep in places. The terrain is mostly open moorland and the route should only be attempted by a fit horse and rider.

There are ample 'watering holes' for your horses along this route, but facilities for riders are not so plentiful. In order to be certain of food and drink, riders are advised to provide a packed meal.

Route Description:

1.   Take the bridleway (GR.773392) to Landacre via Picked Stones. *(You will find the turning to the bridleway opposite the Exmoor Forest Hotel).* At the first cross paths turn left and follow the main track up through the woods. When you reach the top of the woods, turn right and go through a gate to follow the waymarked path through the fields and past Winstichen Farm (GR.784388). Continue to follow the field boundary on your left until you come to a gully. Walk through the gully and turn right downhill and follow the grassy track to the river White Water (GR.796379). Cross the river at the ford and follow the track which goes up the other side. Where the track forks take the right fork and follow it on to Picked Stones Farm (GR.800371). Continue past the farm and turn right off the track through a field to the open moor.

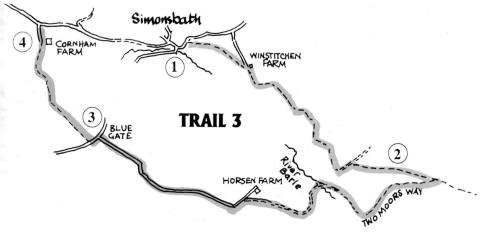

27

2. Ride straight on until the path joins Two Moors Way (GR.818369). Turn right along Two Moors Way and follow the track to the woods. *There are lovely views down to the famous Landacre Bridge on your left.* Ride through the woods and turn left across a ford (GR.797369). Continue along the track to Horsen Farm (GR.784366). At the farm entrance turn left and follow a metalled road to Blue Gate (GR.758376). (Approximately 7 miles).

3. Turn left along the road. After a short distance turn right through a gate and follow the RUPP signposted to Challacombe via Cornham Ford (GR.756375). Follow the track to a river. Cross the river at the ford below the footbridge and go through a gate (GR.749386). Continue along the track towards Cornham Farm.

4. Follow the waymarkings around the farm and turn left along the farm entrance road. At the main road (B3358) turn left. After riding along this road for approximately half a mile, turn right *(through sheep pens)* and follow the bridleway signposted to Exe Head.

5. Ride along the track through the first field and across the centre ditch. After crossing the ditch, turn left and ride along beside it. Ride towards the top right hand corner of the next field and then in the next field, go diagonally towards the top right hand corner (Exe Head) (GR.752415).

6. At Exe Head, turn left and ride through a gate to follow the track to Hoaroak, keeping left along the steep sided valley. *TAKE CARE over the rough stones before you reach the first ford.*

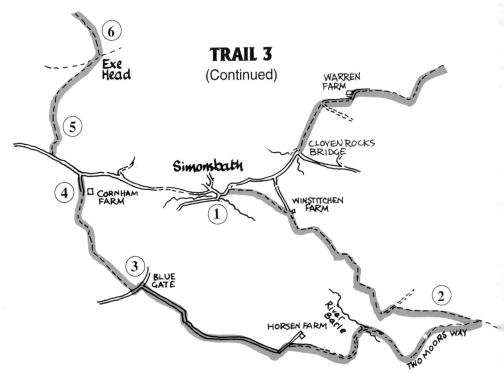

TRAIL 3
(Continued)

7. On reaching Hoaroak (GR.747430), go through a gate and follow the bridleway to Furzehill and Stock Common. (GR.729459). Follow the track past Hoaroak Farmhouse *(which is deserted)* (GR.742435) and then take the feint path which goes uphill to the left. Keep going diagonally over the hill to the left until you come to a gate to the right of a group of trees. Go through the gate and follow the feint, grassy track to the farmland and then, follow the hedge which is on your left, round to the right angled corner and a gate. Go through the gate and keep riding straight on through the fields.

8. When you come to the end of the fields, you will meet a farm lane, and you are now half way along your ride. Go down the lane which is signposted to Cheriton and Sparhanger Cross (GR.729456). At the T-junction of paths, turn right to Cheriton. Follow this track down to cross the river at a ford and up the other side. At the top of the hill, go through a gate and follow the track to the left off the moor (GR.737463). On meeting the road turn right and follow it down the steep hill to come to a T-junction; here turn right to Bridge Ball. Cross the bridge, turn right and ride up through the woods (GR.742469) to a road.

9. Turn right and ride along a metalled road, then, where the road turns sharply right, go through a gate on your left (GR.746464) and follow a bridleway to the moor. On reaching the moor, ride towards the road (B3223) on your left and follow it for 0.75 miles to Dry Bridge. Shortly after Dry Bridge turn left along a track signposted to Doone Valley, Brendon and Malmsmead and follow it across the

moor. Keep following this main track ignoring all turnings until the track divides in a 'Y' (GR.777461). *From here there are lovely views out to your right towards Doone Valley.* Take the left fork signposted to Malmsmead. Ride straight across the next road (GR.781474) and follow the bridleway down through the woods. When you come to a metalled road, turn right, then right again to ride up through the woods to Malmsmead. (Approximately 19 miles).

10. At Malmsmead, turn right (GR.791478) and follow the metalled road round through the ford, then, where the road bends right, you turn left (GR.794478) and follow the bridleway to Oare, turning right after crossing the ford. When you reach the next metalled road, turn right and then left at the T-junction (GR.802473). Ride past the church and immediately after, turn right through a gate (GR.802473) onto a bridleway.

TRAIL 3
(Continued)

29

11.   Follow the bridleway up through fields and out onto the open moor. Keep alongside the fence on your left to go back onto farmland. Now follow

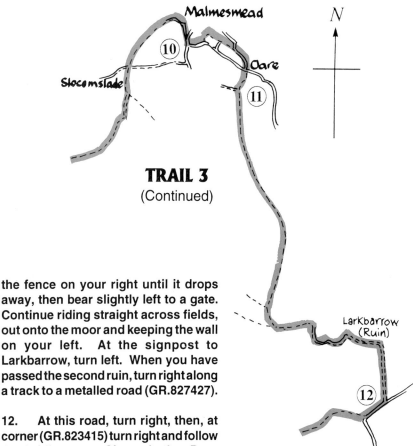

TRAIL 3
(Continued)

the fence on your right until it drops away, then bear slightly left to a gate. Continue riding straight across fields, out onto the moor and keeping the wall on your left.   At the signpost to Larkbarrow, turn left. When you have passed the second ruin, turn right along a track to a metalled road (GR.827427).

12.   At this road, turn right, then, at corner (GR.823415) turn right and follow the bridleway to Simonsbath.   Pass Warren Farm (GR.795408) and follow the track to a river.   Where the track bends sharply left, turn right and go uphill. *GREAT CARE must be taken here as the path is very steep*. Continue riding straight on to Clovenrocks Bridge (GR.786398).   At the main road (B3223) turn right and so return to Simonsbath and your starting point.

Galloy Bridge, Dunster

32

WHEDDON CROSS

A 26 MILE CIRCULAR TRAIL (CLOCKWISE)

Ordnance Survey Map:
Landranger: 181

Parking & Starting Point
Parking is available in the public car park at the back of the Rest & Be Thankful Public House (GR.923388). Your starting point is at the centre of Wheddon Cross (GR.923388).

NOTE: *This trail takes you through varied scenery, open moorland, steeply wooded combes and enclosed farmland. It makes a long day ride and, due to the steep hills, should only be attempted by a fit horse and rider.*

Route Description:

1. From your starting point at the centre of Wheddon Cross, take the minor road signposted towards Cutcombe and then take the second right turn before you reach the church. When you reach the point where the road bends round sharply to the right continue straight on along the rough track (GR.929388). Follow the waymarked path past Pitleigh to the next metalled road (GR.943371).

2. Ride straight across the road and follow the bridleway to Lype Common riding diagonally to the left across the first three fields. PLEASE DO NOT GALLOP THROUGH THE FIELDS. In the fourth field follow the fence on your right and then in the fifth field turn right and ride towards the barns. Leaving the barns on your right, go through a gate and into the forestry plantation. Follow the main forestry track straight on. When

you reach the car park on top of Kennisham Hill (GR.964358), turn right across the main road (B3224) and follow the minor road.

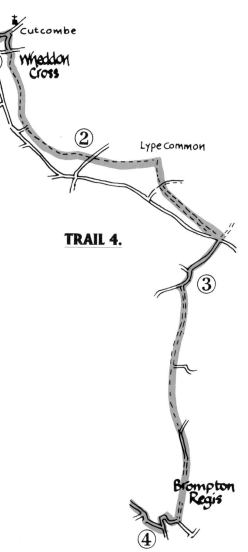

TRAIL 4.

3. Continue along this road past the white house on the right. Around the corner, take the turning on the left signposted to Leigh Farmhouse (the bridleway is signposted to Brompton Regis) (GR.958351). Follow the farm track, then at the right angled bend, carry straight on into the fields towards the corner of the hedge ahead. Follow the field boundary on your left and go through the edge of the wood and then follow the boundary on your right. At the farm track (GR.957328) turn right and follow it to a sharp bend. Turn right down the track and follow it round through the ford (GR.954313). (Approximately 6 miles).

4. When you come to a road, turn right to Brompton Regis. In Brompton Regis (GR.951315), go past the shop, *(ideally situated for stopping to shop with a horse!)*then, where the road bends sharp left, turn right uphill (GR.951315). *Around the corner on your left is The George Public House.* At the next road junction, turn right, then take the next left along the bridleway to Exton and Bridgetown *(this is a metalled farm track)*. Follow this track through two farms and on to the barn on the top of the hill (GR.934330). From here take the bridleway to Bridgetown, keeping the hedge on your left through the first two fields. In the third field turn and ride downhill to the right and follow the track into the woods. At the cross paths, go straight on and follow the path behind the Badgers Holt Public House to the main road (A396).

5. Turn right and ride for a short distance along the road, then take the next turn left. Ride over the two bridges and then turn left between the houses along the bridleway to Hollam Farm (GR.922322). Follow the bank on your right through the first field and go through the gate on your right. From here a grassy lane leads uphill beside the left

hedge and into the woods. At the T-junction in the woods, turn right and then almost immediately left. Go through the left gate follow the hedge on your right to a stony lane. (GR.919324). At the lane, turn right and follow it on round to the right into open fields. In the open fields, follow the hedge on your right until the hedge drops away, then ride towards the beech trees which are straight ahead. Continue to follow the track to a road (GR.915332).

6. Turn left along this road and follow it uphill to Summerway (GR.906331). Go through the gate on your right and follow the right hedge round, towards Spire Cross. Go through the marked gate on your right and follow the waymarked path to a road. Turn right past the Folly *(you will pass the Caratacus Stone, an ancient monument which is protected*

from the weather with a small stone shelter), and follow the road right, then where it bends sharp right (GR.892344), *(your half way point is here),* turn left along the grassy track to Winsford Hill.

7. At the main road (B3223), turn right along the bridleway *(grassy track)* to Withycombe Farm. Leave the open moor and follow the waymarked path down through the fields. *This path runs along the edge of the Punchbowl and is very steep so take care.* Cross the river at the ford (GR.874382) and follow the farm track to a road where you turn right (GR.889354). After 0.25 miles turn left along the bridleway over Bye Common to meet the river.

8. At the river, turn left and follow the bridleway through Nethercote and Lyncombe to Higher Combe (GR.872381). At the T-junction, turn left (GR.874382) and then left again at a road. Ride straight across the main road (B3224) to Stone. *TAKE CARE over the slippery rocks in the lane.* Follow the bridleway across Hoar Moor to a road (GR.854404). (Approximately 19.50 miles).

TRAIL 4
(Continued)

35

9.	Turn right along the road and keep right at the next road junction. After approximately 1.75 miles, turn right along the signposted track, 'Dickie's Path to Webber's Post' *(just before farmland)* (GR.878426). Where the path divides, take the left fork and follow this to meet a road. *There are lovely views of Dunkery Beacon on your right as you ride along here.* At the road, turn right and follow the road uphill for 0.75 miles (GR.904425). Turn left and follow the bridleway diagonally downhill to farmland, then follow the waymarked path downhill to a river (GR.910404). Cross the river at the ford and turn left and follow the bridleway to a road.

10.	Ride straight across the road and follow the bridleway past Raleigh Manor (GR.920395). *This path can become quite muddy at times so take it slowly.* Where the road divides take the right fork to the A396 (GR.925391). Cross straight over the main road and follow the bridleway to Wheddon Cross, keeping the hedge on your left, to come to your starting point.

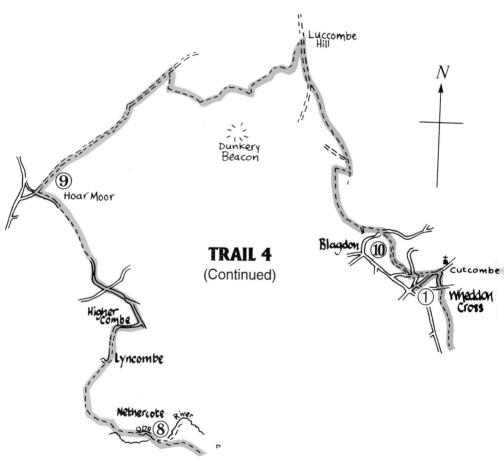

N

Luccombe Hill

Dunkery Beacon

⑨ Hoar Moor

TRAIL 4
(Continued)

Blagdon ⑩

Cutcombe

① Wheddon Cross

Higher Combe

Lyncombe

Nethercote ⑧ River

Mooroak

EXFORD

TRAIL 5

A 21 MILE CIRCULAR TRAIL (CLOCKWISE)

Ordnance Survey Map:
Landranger: 181

Parking & Starting Point:
Parking is available at the public carpark (GR.854383) and your starting point is from the centre of Exford (GR.852385)

NOTE: This trail starts from Exford, a very popular village with its own working forge. It is a hilly route over open moorland and through wooded combes so it should only be tackled by a fit horse and rider.

There are ample 'watering holes' for horses along this route, but facilities for riders are not so plentiful. In order to be certain of food and drink, riders are advised to provide a packed meal.

Route Description:

1.   From your starting point take the bridleway north out of Exford to Dunkery. Climb uphill, and at the T-junction of tracks (GR.855404) turn left to a metalled road. When you reach the road, turn left. Continue on this road until you reach another road junction (GR.851404) where you turn right then take the next left along the bridleway to Almsworthy Common, *(this starts off along a metalled lane).* At Almsworthy Common turn left and follow the track which is parallel with the wall on your left until you come to a road (GR.835422).

2.   At the metalled road, turn right and ride along here for 0.75 miles to Lucott Cross (GR.844432). At Lucott Cross, go straight on along the track which is signposted to Porlock via Lucott. When you reach farmland, go through a gate and follow the field boundary round to the right. Ride through the next gate and follow the track downhill to . Lucott Farm (GR.865450). Go through the farmyard and opposite the last barn, take the narrow stony track on your right, signed to Nutscale (GR.866450). When you reach the hairpin bend, go through the gate on your left and follow the path through the woods to the open moor to come onto a minor road (GR.879446) where you turn left. (Approximately 5.50 miles).

3.   Ride along this minor road for 1 mile and turn right along 'Flora's Ride to Horner Gate' which is opposite a stretch of woodland (GR.890453). When you come to a junction of paths, take the right fork and keep following the higher path for approximately 0.75 miles to a T-junction of paths above woods; here turn left (GR.888443). Enter the woods and follow the track towards Horner Water. At the cross tracks, turn right along the path signposted 'Granny's Ride' and continue downhill to the river (GR.888438), ignoring all side turnings. *The woods are beautiful here but the tracks are very steep and quite tiring for your horse!* At the river, turn right to the ford

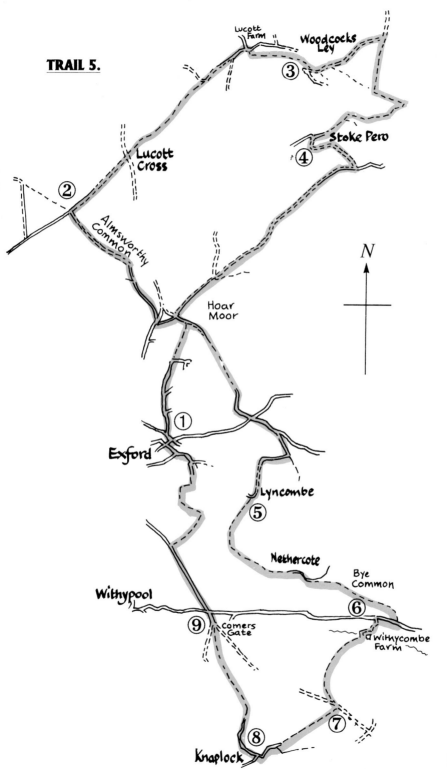

TRAIL 5.

Lucott Farm

Woodcocks Ley

③

Lucott Cross

②

Stoke Pero

④

Almsworthy Common

N

Hoar Moor

①

Exford

Lyncombe

⑤

Nethercote

Bye Common

Withypool

⑥

⑨ Comers Gate

Withycombe Farm

⑦

⑧

Knaplock

39

and cross over the river and retrace your steps to the path which you follow uphill to the next T-junction of paths where you turn right to Stoke Pero (GR.878435). Ride through the farmyard to the metalled road and then turn left.

4. Follow this road to the T-junction and turn right signposted to Exford. Ride straight on along this road for 2 miles to Hoar Moor. *(You are now just over half-way)*. At the cross roads (GR.854405) turn left and follow the RUPP to Stone. *TAKE CARE over the slippery rocks in the lane.* Go straight across the main road (B3224) and follow the minor road for a short distance before taking the first right turn and then the first right again to Lyncombe (GR.868375).

5. Continue to follow the bridleway to Nethercote (GR.874362). Cross the river by the bridge and then turn right uphill over Bye Common. Follow the bridleway to the next road and then turn right (GR.892353).

6. After 0.25 miles take the left turning signposted to Withycombe Farm to follow the bridleway down through the farm, across the river at the ford and up the steep hill on the other side. *This path leads along the edge of the Punchbowl and really is very steep so take care.* Go out onto the open moor again and follow the grassy track to the main road over Winsford Hill (GR.883339).

7. Ride straight across a road and follow the grassy track down towards the farmland which lies straight ahead. Go through the gate into the fields and follow the bank on your right down to a lane leading straight on. Continue along the lane until you come to a T-junction (GR.871332). Turn right along the track to Knaplock. (Approximately 17.50 miles).

8. When you reach Knaplock, turn right and follow the track towards Comer's Gate, to go out again on to the open moor and follow the bank on your left. When the bank drops away to your left, continue to ride straight on across the moor crossing the next track at right angles. Keeping roughly parallel with the farmland on your left, ride straight on for a main road at Comer's Gate (GR.860353) where it passes to the right of a clump of trees.

9. At the main road (B3223), turn left and after approximately 1 mile turn right through a gate into fields and follow the waymarked bridleway to Court Farm (GR.857380). Follow the farm lane back to the road and turn right to Exford and your starting point.

Dunster, one of the best examples of an
English Medieval Village

TRAIL 6

A 60 MILE LONG DISTANCE TRAIL
(CLOCKWISE)

Ordnance Survey Maps:
Landranger 180 & 181

Parking & Starting Points:
Parking is available in the public carpark
in the village of Withypool. Your starting
point is also here at GR.846355

*NOTE: This long distance trail makes a
wonderful riding holiday. Winding its way
thorough the varied Exmoor scenery it
crosses great expanses of open moorland,
climbs through steep wooded combes and
gives tantalizing glimpses of the sea in the
distance. The rider is more than likely to
see wild Red Deer, herds of Exmoor ponies
and many other species of wildlife. The
route can be divided into sections to suit
the individual horse and rider. It should be
borne in mind that the hills in this area are
quite steep when planning your daily ride
and longer distances should only be
tackled by a fit horse and rider. Distances
given in the text have been taken from a
flat map and are therefore only
approximate. To help you to plan your ride
we give the distances, from Withypool, to
the Bed & Breakfast establishments
advertising on this route.*

12 miles	-	*North Furzehill Farm*
16.50 miles	-	*Shilstone Farm*
18 miles	-	*Millslade Country House Hotel*
36 miles	-	*The Dell, Timberscombe*
48 miles	-	*Exford - you have a choice here*

*There are ample 'watering holes' for horses
along this route, but refreshment facilities
for riders are not so plentiful. In order to be*
*certain of food and drink, riders are advised
to provide a packed meal.*

Route Description:

1.   Ride from Withypool and turn
left out of the village just before the
Royal Oak Public House and then take
the next left signposted to the hotel
(Westerclose). Follow this road to the
moor and continue along the track to
meet the next road (GR.824367). Go
straight across the road and follow the
Two Moors Way to the forestry
plantation which is beside the River
Barle (GR.802366). *This is a lovely
section of the ride with views down to
the famous Landacre Bridge on your
left.* Cross the river at the ford
(GR.797369) and continue along the
track to Horsen Farm. At the farm
entrance turn left and follow the
metalled road to Blue Gate.
(Approximately 5.50 miles)

2.   On reaching Blue Gate, turn left
along the metalled road. After a short
distance, turn right through a gate and
follow the RUPP signposted to
Challacombe via Cornham Ford
(GR.756375). Follow the track to meet
the river. Cross the river at the ford
which is below the footbridge and go
through the gate (GR.749386). Continue
to follow the track towards Cornham
Farm (GR.748392).

3.   Follow the waymarkings around
the farm and turn left along the entrance
road. When you meet the main road

43

(B3358) (GR.747395), turn left. Ride along this road for approximately 0.50 miles and turn right (through sheep pens) to follow the bridleway signposted to Exe Head.

4. Ride along the track through the first field and across the centre ditch to turn left and ride along beside it. Ride towards the top right hand corner of the next field and through to the next field where you ride diagonally for the top right hand corner of the field (Exe Head) (GR.752415).

5. At Exe Head turn left through a gate and follow the track to Hoaroak keeping left along the steep sided valley. *TAKE CARE there is rough stone before the first ford.*

6. At Hoaroak (GR.747430) go through the gate and follow the bridleway to Furzehill and Stock Common. Continue along the track past the deserted Hoaroak farmhouse and then take the faint path uphill to the left. Keep riding diagonally over the hill to the left and go towards the gate to the right of a group of trees. Follow the faint grassy track to the farmland and then follow the hedge on your left round to a right-angled corner and a gate. Go through the gate and ride straight on through the fields. (Approximately 11 miles).

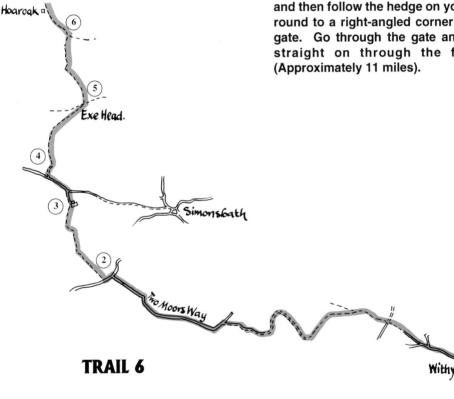

TRAIL 6

44

Brendon

Bridge Ball

Malmsmead

⑨

⑩

Cheriton

Shilstone Hill

⑧

⑦

Brendon Common

Larkbarrow

7.   When you come to the edge of the fields you will meet a farm lane. Go down the lane which is signposted to Cheriton and Sparhanger Cross (GR.729456). At the T-junction of paths turn right to Cheriton. Follow the track steeply down to cross the river at a ford and ride up the other side. At the top of the hill go through a gate and follow the track to the left off the moor (GR.737463). On meeting the road, turn right and follow it down the steep hill to come to a T-junction where you turn right to Bridge Ball. Cross the bridge and turn right up through the woods (GR.742469) to a road.

8.   Turn right along a metalled road and then, where it turns sharply right, go through a gate on your left (GR.746464) and follow a bridleway to the moor. When you reach the moor, ride towards the road (B3223) on your left and follow it for 0.75 miles to Dry Bridge. Shortly after Dry Bridge turn left along a track signposted to Doone Valley, Brendon and Malmsmead and follow this track across the moor. Keep following this main track, ignoring all turnings until the track divides in a 'Y' (GR.777461). *This is Lorna Doone country and there are wonderful views out to your right towards Badgworthy Water and Doone Valley.* Take the left fork signposted to Malmsmead. Ride straight across the next road (GR.781474) and follow the bridleway down through the woods. When you come to a metalled road turn right then right again up through the woods to Malmsmead. (Approximately 16 miles).

9.   At Malmsmead turn right (GR.791478) and follow the road round through a ford, then where the road bends right, turn left (GR. 794478) and follow the bridleway to Oare turning right after crossing the ford. When you come to the next metalled road, turn right and then left at the T-junction (GR.802473). Ride past the church and immediately after, turn right through a gate (GR. 802473) onto a bridleway.

45

10. Follow the bridleway up through the fields and out onto the open moor. Keep alongside the fence on your left and go back onto farmland. Follow the fence on your right until it drops away and then bear slightly left to a gate. Continue to ride straight across fields and out onto the moor keeping the wall on your left. At the signpost to Larkbarrow turn left and from there follow the bridleway to the metalled road at Alderman's Barrow (GR.835422). On reaching this road, turn left and follow the road to Lucott Cross (GR.844432). (Approximately 21 miles).

11. At Lucott Cross ride straight on along the track which is signed to Porlock via Lucott. When you come to farmland, go through a gate and follow the field boundary round to the right. Go through the next gate and follow the track downhill to Lucott Farm (GR.865450). Ride through the farmyard and, opposite the last barn,

take the narrow stony track which is on your right and signed to Nutscale (GR.866450). At the hairpin bend, go through a gate on your left and follow the path through the woods to the open moor to come onto a minor road (GR.879446) where you turn left.

12. Ride along this minor road for one mile and turn right along the signposted 'Flora's Ride to Horner Gate', opposite a stretch of woodland (GR.890453). When you come to a junction of the paths take the right fork and keep following the higher path for approximately 0.75 miles to a T-junction of paths above the woods, turn left (GR.888443). Enter the woods and follow the track towards Horner Water. At a cross-tracks turn right along the path signposted 'Granny's Ride' and continue downhill to the river (GR.888438), ignoring all side turnings. *The woods are beautiful in this area but the hills are very steep and quite tiring for your horse!* At the river, turn right to the ford and cross over to retrace your steps to the path which you follow uphill. At the junction of the paths, turn left and follow the bridleway through fields to Cloutsham (GR.892431) where you turn left and follow the bridleway down to cross the river at the ford and ride up the other side to a road (GR.903433).

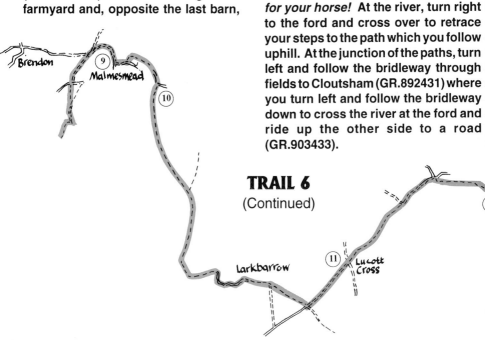

TRAIL 6
(Continued)

3. At this road turn right and keeping left at the next junction GR.902439) follow it to Webber's Post. When you reach Webber's Post GR.903436), turn left and follow the Dunster Path to Brockwell'. Keep ollowing the main path until just before he woods, then turn downhill to your eft (GR.922432). Ride down this track hrough the woods and into the lane unning between the fields. When you each the ford cross and then turn left nd continue along the track to a road. Approximately 29 miles)

4. At the minor road (GR.928431) urn left to Wootton Courtenay. At the ext road junction, turn right. Just efore the houses, turn left uphill and long the bridleway to Dunster GR.937434). *Whilst you are riding long the top, on a clear day there are pectacular views out across Blue nchor Bay.* In Dunster, follow the ridleway past the cemetery to St eorge's Street. Turn right past the chool and then right again along West treet (GR.990435). Turn left after The orester's Public House to Gallox ridge (GR. 989433). Cross the bridge nd follow the bridleway to uxborough. At the next road junction urn left and take the next left along a rack to Broadwood Farm. At the farm, ollow the stream and take the second

turn right. At the next junction (GR.987412) turn left uphill along the bridleway to the forestry track. Almost immediately turn right off the track again and carry straight on through the woods to the next forestry track which leads straight on up over Black Hill. When you come to the next junction of tracks, take the track for Luxborough. On meeting a road turn right and then right again to go through Luxborough village (GR.984377). (Approximately 37 miles).

Take the second road on the right to Dunster. After 0.25 miles take the track on the left which is signposted Wheddon Cross. Cross the stream and turn right and then right again to leave the ponds on your left (GR.981370). Follow the track along the hillside until you come to the fork just before it drops downhill towards a cottage (GR.979369). Take the right fork and follow the waymarked path into the woods. Go through the woods and cross over the river at the ford (GR.973369) and turn left uphill, and at the next junction turn right. *This area is used for pheasant rearing so take care as the young birds may startle your horse!* After a short distance, turn left and follow the waymarked bridleway uphill to the fields. When you reach the field gate, go through and turn right along the field side to the next gate. Go through the gate to the main forestry track.

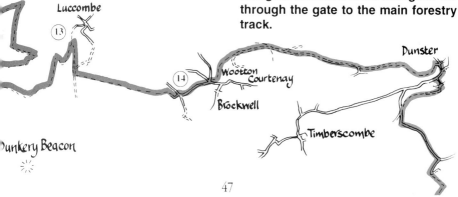

15. At the main forestry track, turn right and follow the track downhill. On reaching the stream, take the bridleway uphill to your left and follow it through the plantation to the next forestry track. Turn left here and at the next junction, turn right to the car park on the top of Kennisham Hill (GR.964358). Turn right here and follow the forestry track straight on to come to a field gate and fields. Go through the gate and ride across the field leaving the barns on your left. At the next junction of paths, turn left and follow the waymarkings through the fields to a road. <u>PLEASE DO NOT GALLOP THROUGH THE FIELDS.</u>

At the road (GR.943371), go straight across and follow the waymarked path past Pitleigh to Wheddon Cross. Go straight on along the road and then take the next turning left (GR.929391). Where the road bends sharp left, go through the gate (GR. 927391) and follow the hedge on the right to come to a main road (A396). Cross straight over the road and follow the lane downhill taking the second turning right along the bridleway to Raleigh Manor (GR.923390). (Approximately 42 miles).

16. Before you reach the manor, turn right and follow the bridleway through the woods keeping along the main track. *This track can become quite muddy at times so take it slowly.* At the next road (GR.918398) go straight across and follow the bridleway through the woods. Just before you come to the stream coming down from the left (GR.911401), turn left and follow the bridleway uphill out of the woods. When you meet a road (GR.906395) turn right and then take the next left to Codsend (GR. 904396). Ride along this road for one mile, go round a sharp bend to the

left, cross the bridge over a river and turn left along a bridleway. After a short distance turn right (GR.887396) uphill along a narrow lane and follow the bridleway to a road (B3224). Turn right along the B3224 for 0.25 miles and then turn right uphill along the bridleway to Kitnor Heath. After approximately 0.50 miles, turn left off the track and follow the bridleway straight on to Prescott Down (GR.862397). On reaching the T-junction of the paths, turn left and follow the RUPP to Stone. *TAKE CARE over slippery rocks in the lane.* Go straight across the B3224 and follow the minor road for a short distance before taking the first right and then the first right again to Lyncombe (GR.868375). (Approximately 47 miles).

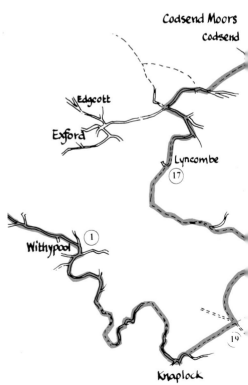

17. Continue to follow the bridleway to Nethercote (GR. 874362). Cross over the river by the bridge and then turn right uphill over Bye Common. Follow the bridleway to the next road and turn right (GR. 892353).

18. Follow this road for 0.25 miles then take the left turning signposted to Withycombe Farm. Continue along the bridleway down through the farm, across the river and up the steep hill on the other side. *This path runs along the edge of what is known as The Punchbowl and really is very steep, so take care.* Go out onto the open moor again and follow the grassy track to a main road over Winsford Hill (GR.883339). (Approximately 51 miles).

19. Go straight across the road and follow the grassy track down towards the farmland straight ahead. Go through the gate into the fields and follow the bank on your right down to a lane. Continue straight on along the lane to the T-junction (GR 871332). Turn right along the track to Knaplock (GR.868331). Turn right and follow the bridleway to Great Bradley (GR 863345). From Great Bradley follow the bridleway to the River Barle. Turn left at the river and follow to the ford near King's Farm (GR 851350). *This is a really lovely section of the ride through the flat, sheltered fields of a typical Exmoor valley.* Cross the river and follow the bridleway up through the farm to come to a road. At this road turn right and follow downhill to Withypool and your starting point.

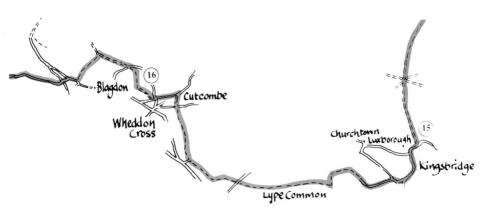

TRAIL 6
(Continued)

THE BRITISH HORSE SOCIETY

The British Horse Society was founded in 1947 when two separate equestrian bodies - The National Horse Association and the Institute of the Horse and Pony Club - decided to join forces and work together for the good of both horse and rider.

It is a marriage that has proved to be a great success and the British Horse Society has steadily increased its membership from just 4000 in the late 1960's to over 60,000 in the 1990's.

By becoming members of the British Horse Society, horse lovers know they are joining a body of people with a shared interest in the horse. Members can be sure that they are contributing to the work of an equine charity with a primary aim to improve the standards of care for horses and ponies. Welfare is not only about the rescuing of horses in distress (which we do); it is also about acting to prevent abuse in the first place. There are many means to achieving this: by teaching and advising, by looking to the horse's well-being and safety, by providing off-road riding, by encouraging high standards in all equestrian establishments, and fighting for the horse's case with government and in Europe.

The British Horse Society works tirelessly towards these aims thanks to the work of its officials at Stoneleigh and its army of dedicated volunteers out in the field.

Membership benefits the horse lover as well as the horse; the Society can offer something to all equestrians, whether they are weekend riders, interested spectators or keen competitors. The benefits include free Third Party Public Liability and Personal Accident insurance, free legal advice, free publications, reductions to British Horse Society events, special facilities at the major shows, and free advice and information on any equine query.

Largely financed by its membership subscriptions, the Society welcomes the support of all horse lovers. If you are thinking of joining the Society and would like to find out more about our work, please contact the Membership Department at the following address:

The British Horse Society
British Equestrian Centre
Stoneleigh Park
Kenilworth
Warwickshire
CV8 2LR
(Telephone: 0203 696697)
Registered Charity No. 210504